MORRILL ELEMENTARY SCHOOL

34880000812201

W9-ASC-148

DEMCO

PROPERTY OF
CHICAGO BOARD OF EDUCATION
DONALD L. MORRILL SCHOOL

HIROSHIMA

PROPERTY OF
CHICAGO BOARD OF EDUCATION
DONALD L. MORRILL SCHOOL

Turning Points in American History

HIROSHIMA

Martin McPhillips

Silver Burdett Company, Morristown, New Jersey

Cincinnati; Glenview, Ill.; San Carlos, Calif.;
Dallas; Atlanta; Agincourt, Ontario

Acknowledgements

We would like to thank the following people for reviewing the manuscript and for their guidance and helpful suggestions: Professor Kenneth Kusmer, Department of History, Temple University; Diane Sielski, Library Media Coordinator, Coldwater Village Exempted Schools, Coldwater, Ohio; and Vincent J. Coffey.

Cover: Photo of the A-Bomb Dome in Hiroshima courtesy of UPI/Bettmann Archive
Title page: Photo of Hiroshima courtesy of UPI/Bettmann Archive
Contents page: Photo of atomic bombshell courtesy of the U.S. Air Force
Page 26: Photo of J. Robert Oppenheimer courtesy of UPI/Bettmann Archive

 Created by Media Projects, Inc.

Series design by Bruce Glassman
Ellen Coffey, Project Manager
Frank L. Kurtz, Project Editor
Jill Hellman, Photo Research Editor

Library of Congress Cataloging-in-Publication Data

McPhillips, Martin, 1950-
   Hiroshima.

   (Turning points in American history)
   Bibliography: p.
   Includes index.
   Summary: Traces the development of the atomic bomb and how the decision was made to drop it on Hiroshima on August 6, 1945. Also discusses the aftermath of that event and its implications for the future of the world.
   1. Hiroshima-shi (Japan) — History — Bombardment, 1945 — Juvenile literature. 2. Atomic bomb — Japan — Hiroshima-shi — History — Juvenile literature. 3. World War, 1939-1945 — Aerial operations, American — Juvenile literature. 4. World politics — 1945-   — Juvenile literature.
   [1. Hiroshima-shi (Japan) — Bombardment, 1945. 2. Atomic bomb — Japan — Hiroshima-shi. 3. World War, 1939-1945 — Aerial operations, American] I. Title. II. Series.
   D767.25.H6M39 1985   940.54'25   85-40170

ISBN 0-382-06976-5 (softcover)
ISBN 0-382-06829-7 (lib. bdg.)

Copyright © 1985 Silver Burdett Company

All rights reserved. No part of this book may be reproduced or utilized in any form, or by any means, electronic or mechanical, including photocopying, recording, or by any information storage or retrieval system, without permission in writing from the Publisher. Inquiries should be addressed to Silver Burdett Company, 250 James Street, Morristown, N.J. 07960.

Published simultaneously in Canada by GLC/Silver Burdett Publishers.

Manufactured in the United States of America.

CONTENTS

INTRODUCTION

A NEW KIND OF WAR

On August 6, 1945, the United States dropped the first nuclear bomb ever used in war. This bomb's target was the Japanese city of Hiroshima. Three days later, the second and last nuclear bomb ever used in war was dropped on Nagasaki, another Japanese city. These bombings ended World War II in Asia, or the "Pacific theater of operations." On August 15, 1945, Japan surrendered unconditionally to the United States and its allies.

World War II was the most wide-ranging and destructive war in human history. Entire countries and great cities were left in ruin. The total loss of life came to some 50 million persons. Many others, soldiers and civilians alike, were wounded and left permanently disabled. Fear and terror were a common reality for millions more.

The atomic bomb was clearly a product of the war. If one looks deeper into the bomb's origins, it can be seen as a product of several centuries of human warfare and human destructiveness. Ironically, it was also the result of one of the world's great scientific achievements.

Hiroshima changed the course of history. It was the first step toward the self-extinction of the human race. Now, with the buildup of the world's nuclear arsenals, the mechanism for extinction is in place. A single spasm of conflict between the United States and the Soviet Union could spell the end of civilization.

The *meaning* of Hiroshima and its aftermath is what is important to us now. Whatever half-truths or even outright falsehoods have attached themselves to the story of Hiroshima, it has a meaning and a truth in itself that can be understood: The time has come to end all war, and that time will be short. Still, it is important to remember that the same capacity to create nuclear weapons is available to solve the world's problems. It is this knowledge that will enable us to face the threat of nuclear warfare with courage.

The world's first manmade nuclear explosion; Alamogordo, New Mexico, July 16, 1945

1

THE WORLD AT WAR AGAIN

On November 11, 1918, Germany agreed to the armistice that ended what was then known as the "Great War." President Woodrow Wilson of the United States called it a war that would "make the world safe for democracy." It was to have been the "war to end all wars." It did not turn out that way.

The Great War is known to us by a more blunt, objective name: World War I. It was a conflict that claimed approximately 10 million lives in combat. Another 20 million were wounded, maimed, or otherwise disabled. It was the first great "modern" war, during which the tank, airplane, submarine, and poison gas played important combat roles for the first time.

Much of World War I was fought from trenches dug along the lines of battle. Thousands of men, attempting to capture territory, would charge out of

Pearl Harbor, Hawaii; December 7, 1941

their trenches toward the lines of the opposing army, into the teeth of machine-gun and rifle fire, through hedgerows of barbed wire. "No-man's-land" was the name soldiers gave to the territory between trenches.

In a war infamous for the wholesale slaughter of human life, the Battle of Verdun stands out as an event of particularly grisly consequences. Fought between the French and the Germans in 1916 in northeastern France, it lasted for about ten months. The Germans launched a massive offensive against the French lines. The attack was somewhat successful at first, but the French rallied behind the battle cry "They shall not pass." The French then regained the territory the Germans had taken. The battle ended in a virtual stalemate. The losses for both sides came to 680,000 men.

The causes of World War I are still the subject of debate. The spark that ignited it was the assassination of Archduke Ferdinand of Austria-Hungary by a Serbian nationalist—one of a faction who sought to separate the Slavic region of Serbia from the Austro-Hungarian Empire. Rivalries among the nations of Europe had made the continent ripe for conflict, and soon after the assassination, the major powers began declaring war on one another. Once the great military forces of Europe were set in motion, they were seemingly impossible to stop. The Allied Powers of England, France, and Russia on one side and the Central Powers of Germany, Austria-Hungary, and Italy on the other threw themselves into a conflict larger than any the world had yet imagined.

At the war's end, the map of Europe was redrawn. An old order had been swept out of power. New countries were formed. Many borders shifted. The Russian Revolution in 1917 installed the world's first communist dictatorship. And the United States, joining in on the side of the Allies near the end of the war, stepped forward as a great world power.

The First World War did bring about great changes, but was the world better off? Inevitably, yes, some circumstances had improved, but these improvements were short-lived. The political crisis in Europe that had caused World War I was not settled by it. More trouble was waiting down the road.

The 1919 Treaty of Versailles, one of five treaties known as the Peace of Paris

President Woodrow Wilson addressing U.S. troops in Belgium in 1919 shortly after the armistice that ended World War I

UPI/Bettmann Archive

that settled World War I, contributed to the tensions that would lead to the next war. Germany, the big loser, had been drained financially by the cost of the war. The Versailles treaty complicated Germany's economic crisis by requiring it to pay reparations to France, Britain, and the United States. These payments were, in a sense, huge international fines. Germany also lost one seventh of its land, most of it to France and Poland, and all of its foreign colonies. The German economy was shattered.

During the mid-1920s, Germany gradually recovered economic vigor. Then, in 1929, came the crash of the American stock market. Just as the assassination of Archduke Ferdinand had spiraled into world war, the stock-market crash spiraled into a great world economic crisis. In Germany, rapid inflation of paper money and massive unemployment again destroyed the economy.

From the despair and confusion, a political fanatic rose to power on a wave of violence and fear. Adolf Hitler, through the instrument of the Nazi (National Socialist) party, silenced his critics with threats and thuggery. In 1933, Hitler was appointed chancellor of the German Reich by President Hindenburg, who had defeated Hitler in the presidential election of 1932. Hindenburg died the next year, and Hitler was granted dictatorial powers in Germany for a period of four years. He was now free to put into action a perverse plan for the future of Germany.

Hitler used the humiliation that Germany had suffered after World War I to incite the anger and pride of the German people. He virtually hypnotized the nation with a vision of German racial supremacy and world power. By seizing control of nearly every aspect of German life, including education and industry, and by beginning a massive buildup of the military, Hitler resurrected the German economy. This feat brought him great acclaim as a leader. Many prominent people around the world, including in the United States, credited him with a near miracle.

By 1936, Hitler was asserting German power in Europe. He ordered troops to occupy the Rhineland, an area near the French border that the Treaty of Versailles forbade the Germans to fortify. The French and British offered little resistance.

In the meantime, on the other side of the world, Japan was gradually coming under the control of a strong military establishment. In 1931, the Japanese pressed their quest for empire by invading and occupying Manchuria, the great region of northeastern China. This satisfied Japan until 1937, when it began an invasion of China on a much larger scale.

Although Japan is only about the size of the state of California, by the 1930s its population had reached almost 90 million. (At that time, the entire United States had a population of only 127 million.) Japan explained that it was expanding into China to protect China

UPI/Bettmann Archive

Newly appointed chancellor Adolf Hitler and President Paul von Hindenburg, 1933

from communism and from domination by European and American interests. Several major Chinese cities fell to the Japanese, and the hallmark of the invasion was its brutality. As many as 300,000 Chinese civilians were slaughtered.

U.S. president Franklin Delano Roosevelt condemned the Japanese invasion of China, as did the League of Nations, forerunner of the United Nations. Roosevelt linked Japanese aggression to the building militarism of Nazi Germany. He was not making a hollow compari-

son. In 1940, the Japanese joined in the Axis Alliance with Germany and Italy.

In Europe, Hitler was well along in the execution of his plan of conquest. In 1938, he ordered troops into Austria and then annexed that country to the German Reich. Later that year, Hitler entered into the Munich Pact, an agreement with Britain and France that allowed him to annex the Sudetenland, part of Czechoslovakia. Neville Chamberlain, prime minister of Great Britain, declared that the agreement would bring "peace in our time." This policy of "appeasement" was beginning to be viewed by some French and British as an attempt to buy peace by giving in to aggression. Six months later, in March 1939, Hitler occupied the rest of Czechoslovakia, in violation of the Munich agreement. Britain and France objected diplomatically but took no action.

Finally, on September 1, 1939, the German army and air force invaded Poland. Hitler had by then signed a "mutual nonaggression pact" with the Soviet Union, which charged into Poland from the east a few weeks later. The two invaders divided the fallen country between them.

Britain and France, which had sworn to protect Poland's sovereignty, had gone as far as they could to appease Hitler. Now they declared war. The United States was still officially neutral, but it was expected—and hoped—that U.S. involvement in the war would come with time.

Early in 1940, Germany rushed occupation forces into Denmark and Norway. On May 10, they launched their "blitzkrieg," or "lightning war," on Belgium, the Netherlands, and Luxembourg, winning quick victory over all three. A week later the blitzkrieg descended on France. The German advance went virtually unchecked. Ultimate disaster was narrowly averted when the British troops sent to fight in northern France were cornered by the Germans at Dunkirk. Last-minute evacuation of British troops across the En-

glish Channel spared them annihilation. Even so, the British suffered heavy casualties and were forced to abandon an enormous amount of artillery and other matériel.

Less than two weeks later, the Germans occupied Paris. France surrendered shortly thereafter, and on June 22, Hitler danced a jig for photographers to celebrate a stunning victory over an old foe.

But Hitler had far less reason to dance than he might have supposed. The man who had pursued the policy of appeasement, Neville Chamberlain, had resigned as prime minister of Great Britain. In his place came a most formidable leader, outspoken to the extreme in his opposition to the Nazis. Winston Churchill's leadership strengthened the British will. Whatever the price of avoiding defeat, Churchill was determined that Great Britain should pay it.

Hitler was not, to begin with, enthusiastic about a struggle with Britain. But as long as that country resisted his efforts to conquer the European continent, it had to be subdued. Hitler was probably willing to make a deal with Churchill, but Churchill, who could not stomach the barbaric evil of the Nazis, would make no deals.

With the momentum of the war overwhelmingly in his favor, Hitler attacked Great Britain. His plan was to cripple Britain with aerial bombardment and then invade. From mid-August 1940 to the end of September, the Germans con-

September 1938. Hitler and British prime minister Neville Chamberlain discuss German claims in Austria and Czechoslovakia at Hilter's home in Berchtesgaden, not far from Munich. At Chamberlain's right is Joachim von Ribbentrop, the German foreign minister.

ducted regular and heavy bombing of British cities and military targets. But the defending Royal Air Force inflicted heavy losses on the German air force— the famous Luftwaffe—and Hitler was forced to delay and then postpone the invasion. For the first time, he had failed to gain a victory.

With the blitzkrieg stalled at the gates of Britain, the Germans turned their aggression on Eastern Europe and North Africa. Italy entered the war as Germany's ally, and then invaded Greece and Albania.

On June 22, 1941, Hitler's madness

finally led him down the path of his ultimate undoing. He launched a surprise invasion of Russia, thus violating their nonaggression pact of two years before. The Russians were badly prepared, and the blitzkrieg quickly devoured vast regions of Russian territory. Over the following months, however, the resistance of the Russian people and their military toughened. The Germans captured many Soviet men and much equipment and slaughtered hundreds of thousands of civilians, but the Russians inflicted many casualties in return.

Since the invasion of Poland, pres-

UPI/Bettmann Archive

sure had mounted for the United States to join the war. Conservative and isolationist forces within the U.S. strenuously opposed involvement. There was, however, an equally strong feeling that America could not afford to remain neutral. President Roosevelt questioned whether the continents of North and South America would be secure if the Nazis gained an invincible hold on all of Europe.

During this period, relations between the United States and Japan also deteriorated rapidly. Intense diplomatic negotiations between the two countries failed to resolve American objections to ongoing Japanese aggression in Asia.

On December 7, 1941, these tensions came to a head when Japan launched a surprise air attack on the American naval base at Pearl Harbor, Hawaii. During the two-hour raid, 18 major warships of the American Pacific fleet and 349 aircraft were lost or damaged. More than 3,500 men were killed or wounded.

The United States and Great Britain declared war on Japan the next day. A few days later, Japan's allies, Germany and Italy, declared war on the United States. The great industrial power of America would be tested in a two-front war.

The Japanese had put an enormous dent in the existing American war machine. While the Americans were busy restoring their damaged fleet, the Japanese gained a remarkable grip on the Pacific and the Far East. Over the weeks and months following Pearl Harbor, the Japanese moved rapidly and captured the Philippines, Borneo, Hong Kong, Singapore, Malaysia, and New Guinea.

It was not until May 1942 that the Japanese surge was first halted by the United States at the Battle of Midway Island. One reason for the victory was that the Americans had broken the Japanese secret code, and the American high command knew the enemy's strategy in advance. Throughout the war, knowledge of the code would give the Americans a hidden advantage.

National Archives

Hideki Tojo, prime minister of Japan

UPI/Bettmann Archive

American and Filipino prisoners at Bataan after the Japanese occupation of the Philippines in early 1942

The major responsibility for commanding the American forces in the Pacific was divided between Admiral Chester Nimitz and General Douglas MacArthur. It was Nimitz's job to cross the central Pacific toward Japan with naval forces and marines, and MacArthur was to proceed with army troops north from Australia up the island chain to Japan. This division of responsibility led to an unforeseen advantage for the U.S.: The advances of the one force tended to support the other as time went on, and the Japanese could never concentrate their forces to meet one attacking thrust.

By the autumn of 1942, the Americans were fighting a major battle with the Japanese at Guadalcanal, in the Solomon Islands. The Japanese grimly established themselves as tough and unyielding combatants. By early 1943, however, they were finally ready to evacuate Guadalcanal. They had lost 65 naval vessels and more than 800 aircraft.

Because of the greater economic resources of the United States, by 1943 the balance of naval forces had shifted decisively in favor of the U.S. The Japanese could no longer meet the Americans in naval battle, and all their outlying island garrisons became isolated. American commanders were able to concentrate an overwhelming force against any island the U.S. chose to invade.

National Archives

Admiral Chester Nimitz, commander of the Pacific fleet

National Archives

U.S. aircraft carrier following an air strike at the Battle of Midway. This was the only U.S. ship lost during the battle, whereas U.S. pilots sank four Japanese carriers, severely weakening the enemy's already smaller fleet.

A few weeks before the American victory at Guadalcanal, Roosevelt and Churchill met in the Moroccan city of Casablanca. Joseph Stalin, the other member of the "Big Three," could not attend the meeting because of intense fighting in Russia.

As the Casablanca Conference began, the tide was already turning against the Germans in Russia and North Africa. Churchill and Roosevelt agreed to launch a massive invasion of Europe the following year. They also decided that only "unconditional surrender" on the part of the Axis powers would end the war. This decision would not only determine the ultimate conduct of the war but would also affect the shape of the postwar world. A diplomatic solution or an armistice, such as the one that ended World War I, was out of the question. The enemy must be sent down to total defeat. There would be no compromise.

By the middle of 1943, the Soviet Army had captured the momentum along the eastern front, and the Amer-icans had invaded Italy from the south. In early September, the Italians asked for terms of surrender. But the Germans ruthlessly disarmed the Italian army and continued to occupy and defend Italy against the Allied offensive. In northern Europe, the British and Americans joined in stepped-up bombing raids against military targets in Germany. This was in preparation for the major invasion, now rescheduled for mid-1944.

With the campaigns in both Europe and the Pacific going well, victory could be sensed, though it was not yet certain. The war could be won, but the cost in lives and arms was going to be high.

While the war seemed to be headed toward an inevitable Allied victory, new developments had occurred behind the scenes. Scientific discoveries known to both sides had spurred top-secret work on new weapons. Among these new weapons was one with enormous destructive force, something the world had never seen nor hardly imagined.

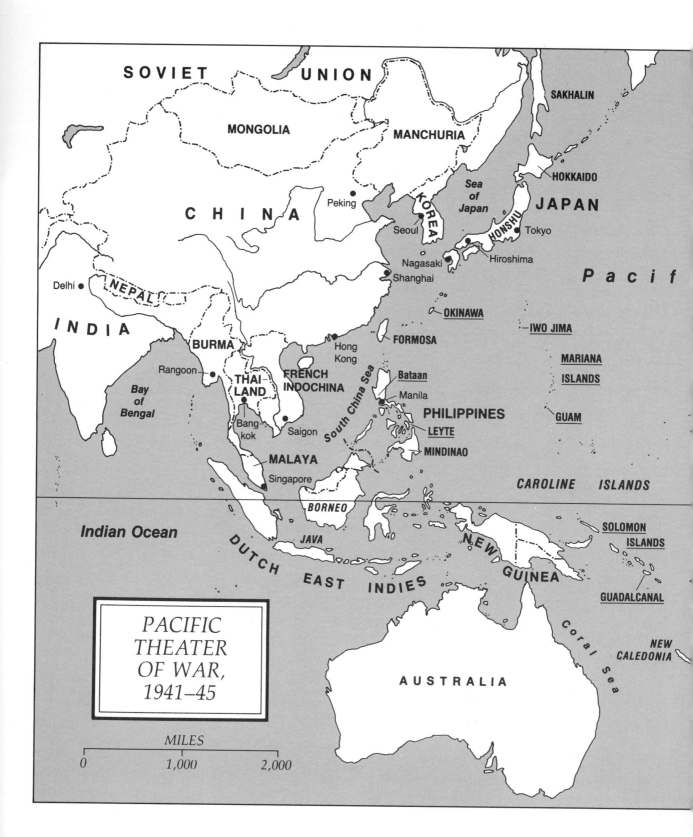

SOVIET   UNION
                                              SAKHALIN
        MONGOLIA   MANCHURIA

                                              HOKKAIDO

     C H I N A   Sea   JAPAN
                     Peking   of
                                        Japan   Tokyo
                              KOREA   HONSHU
                              Seoul   Hiroshima
                                     Nagasaki
Delhi   NEPAL   Shanghai   P a c i f
INDIA
                                                OKINAWA
        BURMA   FORMOSA   IWO JIMA

Rangoon   THAI-   FRENCH   Hong   MARIANA
    Bay of   LAND   INDOCHINA Kong   ISLANDS
    Bengal   Bataan
            Bang-   Manila   GUAM
            kok   Saigon   South China Sea PHILIPPINES
        MALAYA   LEYTE
            Singapore   MINDINAO
                                              CAROLINE   ISLANDS
    Indian Ocean   DUTCH   BORNEO
                                                      SOLOMON
                    EAST   JAVA   NEW   ISLANDS
                        INDIES   GUINEA
                                                      GUADALCANAL

                                                      NEW
                                              Coral   CALEDONIA
        PACIFIC   Sea
        THEATER   AUSTRALIA
        OF WAR,
        1941–45

            MILES
        0   1,000   2,000

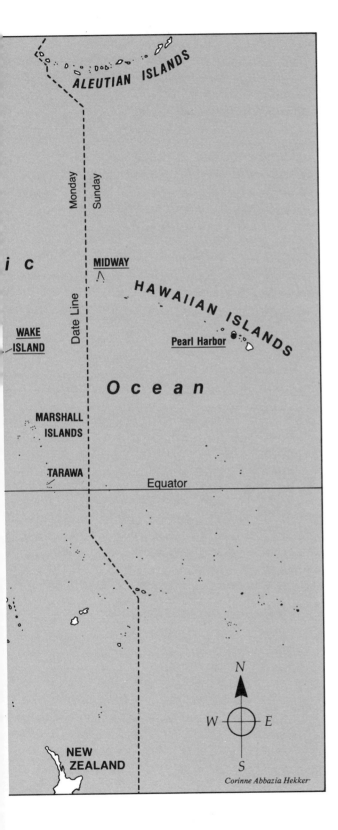

A Brief Chronology

1941

Dec. Japan attacks Pearl Harbor; invades Philippines, Hong Kong, Malaya, Mariana Islands, Burma, Wake Island.

1942

Jan.–Feb. Japan attacks Dutch East Indies; captures Singapore.

April–May. U.S. surrender of Bataan and Corregidor, in the Philippines.

May–June. Japan repulsed at Battles of Coral Sea and Midway.

August. U.S. attacks Japanese positions on Solomon Islands, including Guadalcanal.

1943

Feb. Japan evacuates Guadalcanal.

June. U.S. attacks Japanese positions in New Guinea.

Dec. U.S. assault on Marshall Islands.

1944

June. U.S. begins B-29 bomber raids on Japanese home islands.

Aug. U.S. recovery of Guam and Tinian, in Mariana Islands.

Sept. Allied counteroffensive in Burma.

Oct. Return of U.S. forces to Philippines; Battle of Leyte Gulf.

1945

Feb.–March. U.S. secures Philippines; captures Iwo Jima.

April. U.S. invades Okinawa.

Aug. 6. Atomic bombing of Hiroshima.

Aug. 9. Atomic bombing of Nagasaki.

Aug. 14. Japanese surrender.

19

The United States has only very poor ores of uranium in moderate . . . .
quantities. There is some good ore in Canada and the former Czechoslovakia,
while the most important source of uranium is Belgian Congo.

In view of this situation you may think it desirable to have some
permanent contact maintained between the Administration and the group
of physicists working on chain reactions in America. One possible way
of achieving this might be for you to entrust with this task a person
who has your confidence and who could perhaps serve in an inofficial
capacity. His task might comprise the following:

a) to approach Government Departments, keep them informed of the
further development, and put forward recommendations for Government action,
giving particular attention to the problem of securing a supply of uranium ore for the United States;

b) to speed up the experimental work,which is at present being carried on within the limits of the budgets of University laboratories, by
providing funds, if such funds be required, through his contacts with
private persons who are willing to make contributions for this cause,
and perhaps also by obtaining the co-operation of industrial laboratories
which have the necessary equipment.

I understand that Germany has actually stopped the sale of uranium
from the Czechoslovakian mines which she has taken over. That she should
have taken such early action might perhaps be understood on the ground
that the son of the German Under-Secretary of State, von Weizsäcker, is
attached to the Kaiser-Wilhelm-Institut in Berlin where some of the
American work on uranium is now being repeated.

Yours very truly,

A. Einstein

(Albert Einstein)

2

THE BOMB

On October 11, 1939, just forty-one days after the Germans invaded Poland, Franklin Roosevelt was visited at the White House by Dr. Alfred Sachs, an economist. Sachs, who often advised Roosevelt, hand-delivered a letter from the world's most famous scientist, Albert Einstein.

Einstein wanted to alert Roosevelt to a recent discovery in physics, one that might lead to the development of an extremely powerful bomb. Unfortunately, Einstein explained, the Nazis also knew that such a bomb was possible. Einstein urged Roosevelt to give the matter serious attention.

The new scientific discovery was that the nucleus of an atom could be split, thus converting matter into energy of unearthly proportions. Einstein had first described the relationship of energy to matter in 1905 in his Theory of Special Relativity. But Einstein had not guessed that the atomic nucleus could be split. This first occurred to another free-thinking scientist, Leo Szilard. Szilard was a refugee from Hungary who had imagined an atomic "chain reaction" while watching a traffic light change. Szilard, ironically, was not the first scientist to accomplish nuclear "fission"—the splitting of the atomic nucleus. That happened unexpectedly during an experiment in the laboratory of Otto Hahn, a German scientist working in Berlin.

Hahn bombarded uranium with neutrons and became perplexed when some of the uranium changed into barium, another element. This defied the seemingly unshakable law of physics that matter could be neither created nor destroyed. Another scientist, Lise Meitner, interpreted the experiment for Hahn. She told him that he had split atomic nuclei.

Second page of the letter from Albert Einstein and Leo Szilard to President Roosevelt, urging him to sponsor atomic research. The letter was dated August 2, 1939, and signed only by Einstein.

Roosevelt Library/Hyde Park

Niels Bohr Library/AIP

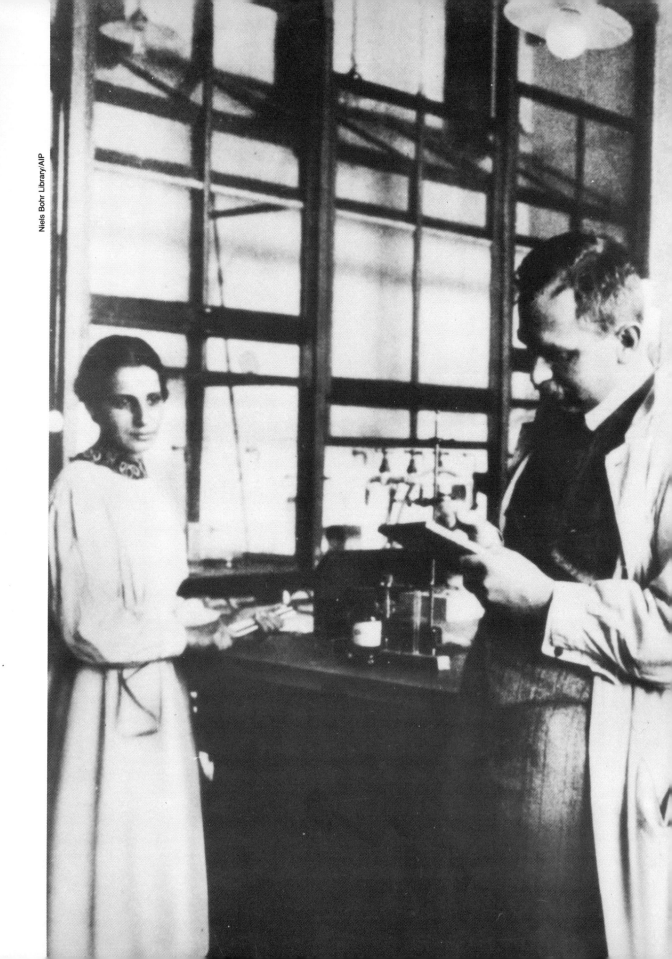

G. W. Szilard/AIP

Albert Einstein and Leo Szilard at work on the letter to President Roosevelt

A handful of the world's physicists began to consider Hahn's experiment with enthusiasm. Szilard led the discussion among the European scientists who, like himself, had fled to the United States to escape the grasp of the Nazis.

Lise Meitner and Otto Hahn at Hahn's laboratory in Berlin. Meitner, who was Jewish, was not present during the experiment itself, having fled to Sweden earlier in 1938 under the threat of Nazi persecution. Her interpretation of the experiment was delivered by mail.

It was Szilard who convinced Einstein that the United States needed to make a major commitment to atomic research. Szilard drafted the letter that Einstein had sent to Roosevelt via Alfred Sachs.

Even with the promise of a super-weapon, and Roosevelt's positive reaction to Einstein's letter, the government did not plunge into development of a bomb. Some work began in New York and Chicago and in Berkeley, California, but great progress was not made.

The atomic scientists in the United

States knew that there were very able scientists still working in Germany who were aware of Otto Hahn's breakthrough. The fear that Hitler might soon possess a superweapon increased until the American government finally committed itself to making the bomb. In 1942, the project was placed in the hands of a brusque, wide-bodied, get-it-done army man.

When he received his new assignment, Colonel Leslie Groves was finishing up the most important project of his career, the construction of the Pentagon. A West Point graduate, Groves's greatest desire was to hold a combat command. He did not really want the A-bomb project. To soothe his disappointment, the army made Groves a general.

Colonel Leslie Groves

Groves attacked the new job with energy and enthusiasm. He met with the scientists across the country involved in nuclear research. The scientists and Groves, as a rule, took an immediate dislike to one another. To Groves the scientists were undisciplined and far afield from practical matters. To the scientists, Groves was a pugnacious bully. The methods of scientific genius and military efficiency appeared totally incompatible.

But somehow it proved to be just the right combination. In his gruff manner, Groves pulled the project together. Over many objections, he appointed a brilliant scientist from Berkeley, Robert Oppenheimer, to be the project director. Oppenheimer proved to be an able handler of the many formidable scientists who worked on the project. Through a combination of charm and his own remarkable intelligence, Oppenheimer was more than a match for the difficult personalities that made up this most impressive collection of scientific genius.

In early 1943, Groves and Oppenheimer moved the team of scientists to seclusion in Los Alamos, New Mexico. There, the "Manhattan Project"—named after the location of the army's first office for atomic research—surged forward under tight security. At the time, haunted by the vision of a world controlled by Nazis equipped with A-bombs, the project seemed to move much too slowly. In real scientific terms,

24

Niels Bohr Library/AIP

Oppenheimer (center) with colleagues at his home in Los Alamos

the accomplishments of the Manhattan Project were remarkable.

While the scientists labored with many complex theoretical and technical problems at their secret compound, factories at Oak Ridge, Tennessee, and Hanford, Washington, were busy producing the radioactive elements needed for the bombs. The plant at Oak Ridge made uranium-235 while the plant in Hanford produced plutonium.

The goal of the Manhattan Project was to have a bomb ready by mid-1945. In Washington, D.C., the policy makers were considering how the bomb could be used to shorten the war. Aware of the bomb's potential for destruction, the advisers to President Roosevelt began to consider its moral and political implications. That the bomb would forever

J. Robert Oppenheimer

No scientist contributed more to the development of the atomic bomb than did J. Robert Oppenheimer, the brilliant theoretical physicist whom General Leslie Groves appointed director of the project. Recruited from the faculty of the University of California at Berkeley, Oppenheimer was also to become the most controversial member of the Los Alamos team.

Success in science came early to Oppenheimer. At the age of eleven, a paper he'd written was delivered before the New York Mineralogical Society by the prodigy himself. And by his mid-twenties, Oppenheimer had become famous for his work in the advancement of physics and for the popularity of the courses he taught at Berkeley.

Like many intellectuals of his generation, Oppenheimer supported such "leftist" or "socialist" causes as aid for the Depression poor and opposition to the fascist insurrection in Spain in 1936. His support for the latter arose in part from his anti-fascist "fury" at the experiences of Jewish relatives who'd been persecuted by fascists in Germany.

Oppenheimer himself was never a member of the Communist Party of the United States, but many of his colleagues at Berkeley were, as were his wife, his brother, and his sister-in-law. In 1943, while Oppenheimer was at work on the Manhattan Project, a fellow Berkeley professor and close friend, Haakon Chevalier, mentioned to him that a mutual friend could secretly transmit technical information to the Soviet Union. Oppenheimer did not report this overture to his superior, General Groves, until several months later.

In a 1953 investigation, the delay in reporting the Chevalier conversation, along with other questions about his loyalties, resulted in Oppenheimer's suspension from the U.S. Atomic Energy Commission on the grounds that he was a "security risk." The investigating board reported that it had found "no indication of disloyalty . . . but fundamental defects in his character."

Like many who worked on the Los Alamos project, J. Robert Oppenheimer had deeply conflicted feelings about the use of the bomb and about its future. Once, at a White House conference, he exclaimed to Harry S. Truman, "Mr. President, I have blood on my hands." On the other hand, he later asserted, "My own view is that the development of atomic weapons . . . can make the problem [of achieving peace] more hopeful . . . because it intensifies the urgency of our hopes—in frank words, because we are scared."

change the nature of war was just becoming clear. And beyond the war effort against Germany and Japan, this new source of military strength could be seen in relation to another country. It was already becoming clear that the Soviet Union, now an ally, would emerge after the war as a great world power, and an adversary.

On June 5, 1944, the long-planned and often-delayed Allied invasion of Europe began. Under the direction of the Supreme Allied Commander, General Dwight D. Eisenhower, the D-Day land-

Enrico Fermi, chief of experimentation at Los Alamos

ing on the Normandy beaches in France was a calculated success. On the eastern front of Europe, the Russians continued to drive the Germans back, and in Italy, the British and Americans continued their sweep north. The new invasion through France virtually assured the destruction of Germany. The Allies were well along the road to victory in Europe.

In the Pacific, U.S. Navy and Marine forces were slowly closing a circle around Japan. But as time went on, especially in the case of the Coral Islands of the central Pacific, each succeeding invasion became more costly for the U.S. as the Japanese dug themselves in, fighting tenaciously on the defensive from tunnels and prepared positions. In the southwest Pacific, MacArthur retook New Guinea and the Solomons in 1943. Eventually, by the fall of 1944, he recaptured the Philippines. During the latter campaign, the already crippled Japanese fleet was almost completely annihilated at the Battle of Leyte Gulf.

More and more American bombers were attacking Japan. Because the bombers were suffering losses, it was decided to attack Iwo Jima in early 1945, so that a landing strip could be built there to service crippled B-29s. This proved to be the most costly invasion yet. The Japanese by this time had developed their defensive tactics to perfection. Also, they had begun to hit U.S. ships with *kamikaze* attacks, in which planes loaded with dynamite were crashed into American ships by pilots

University of Chicago/AIP

American Institute of Physics

Hans Bethe, the Manhattan Project's principal theoretician

willing to commit suicide. The Japanese, it seemed, would never surrender, would have to be blasted out of their defenses. And because of their willingness to sacrifice themselves in suicide missions, there was a belief among U.S. military leaders that if they invaded the home islands of Japan, they would face a bloodbath in which they could suffer a very high number of casualties. This seemed to be borne out in March of 1945, when the U.S. invaded Okinawa, in order to set up a staging point for an invasion of the main Japanese islands. The Japanese garrison of 100,000 men fought

almost to the last man, joined by a great number of Japanese civilians, many of whom committed suicide to avoid capture. The American high command began to wonder what it would finally take to invade and conquer the Japanese mainland.

By early 1945, the Allies had put the squeeze on Germany. Relentless aerial bombardment of major German cities was matched by advancing armies on the ground. In mid-February British and American planes carried out the most destructive and ruthless bombing of the war. Hundreds of bombers dropped tons of both high-explosive bombs and fire bombs (called "incendiary bombs") on the German city of Dresden. Dresden was not a military target but a center for refugees from other war-torn areas of Germany.

For four days and nights, a raging fire storm consumed the city of Dresden. Even the asphalt street paving melted and caught fire. The number of dead was estimated at 130,000. It was probably the largest death toll for any bombing of the war.

By the end of March, the Allies had crossed the Rhine River and invaded Germany. The Russians were grinding away relentlessly from the east.

Back in the United States, with victory in Germany all but complete, attention turned to the invasion of Japan. In the planning stages was a conventional air, sea, and land invasion. But the option of ending it all with the atomic bomb was getting closer to becoming a reality. If the scientists at Los Alamos had the bomb ready in time, the decision would be up to President Franklin Roosevelt. He had been commander in chief throughout the war and had approved the $2 billion effort to develop the weapon.

Roosevelt was never to make that final decision. Elected to an unprecedented fourth term as president in November 1944, he was a man in rapidly declining health. On April 12, 1945, not quite three months after his fourth inauguration, Roosevelt died at his retreat in Warm Springs, Georgia.

As the nation mourned the loss of a beloved leader, the presidency passed to a tough little man from Independence, Missouri. Harry S. Truman had just begun his first term as vice-president. Before that he had served in the Senate. A few days after assuming the presidency, Truman told a gathering of reporters, "Boys, if you ever pray, pray for me now."

3

THE HORROR

During the first days and weeks of his presidency, Harry Truman faced both positive and negative situations. On the plus side, the war in Europe was just about won. And, of great importance, the American people were confident that the national war effort was a success. On the minus side, however, was the declining prospect of an early defeat of Japan, an enemy with too much pride to surrender.

Another troubling situation involved the Russians. After driving the German army out of the Soviet Union, the Russians had their eyes trained keenly on the postwar balance of power. During February 1945, at a conference at Yalta, in the Ukraine, Roosevelt, British prime minister Winston Churchill, and Soviet premier Joseph Stalin had reached agreement on the organization of post-

Some of the destruction in Hiroshima, near "ground zero," the bomb's target

war Europe. Even though Roosevelt and Churchill had conceded a great deal of territory to the Soviet sphere of influence, it was not long before Stalin began violating the Yalta agreements. Specifically, he seized control of beleaguered Poland and put an end to hopes that a new government would be established there through democratic elections.

The day that Harry Truman was sworn in as president was, remarkably, the first day that he heard about the atomic-bomb project. Roosevelt had never included Truman in the inner circle of political leadership who knew about the bomb.

The bomb was still not ready. It had not even been tested. But Truman soon realized that when it was ready, it could be used to bring Japan to its knees without an invasion, an invasion that General George Marshall, the Army chief of staff, had told him could cost half a million or more American lives.

On April 30, only eighteen days after

UPI/Bettmann Archive

Churchill, Roosevelt, and Stalin at the Yalta Conference, February 1945, just two months before Roosevelt's death

Roosevelt's death and Truman's succession, Adolf Hitler committed suicide in his Berlin bunker. The German capital was under siege by the Allies. On May 9, Truman declared victory in Europe.

As these events took place, a special committee appointed by Truman was busy considering the bomb and its use. Headed by Henry Stimson, the aging Secretary of War, the committee was finally to determine how the bomb could best be used to end the war. The scientists at Los Alamos were saying that a bomb could be tested in New Mexico by mid-July. By August 1, a bomb would be ready for use against Japan. Stim-

son's committee had to weigh the options.

Stimson was fully aware of the bomb's destructive force, as aware as anyone could be before the weapon had actually been tested or used. He knew that its very existence threatened the future of civilization. It is believed that the bomb greatly troubled Stimson. He was seventy-eight years old and weary from having managed the most massive war effort in the nation's history. He was growing somewhat frail, and a good night's sleep was a rare pleasure for him. No doubt his troubled sleep was in part caused by this horrible new instrument of war over which he exerted so much control. It was Stimson, perhaps, who best understood the dark side of a victory won with the bomb.

As Secretary of War, however, Stimson had also read the casualty reports, and he knew the tenacious character of the Japanese militarists. The Joint Chiefs of Staff of the U.S. armed forces had said that the invasion of Japan could begin on November 1. The Americans were already softening Japan with continuous aerial bombardment of Tokyo and other major targets. The defeat of Japan by way of an invasion would mean massive destruction. The casualties on both sides, including hundreds of thousands of Japanese civilians, would be enormous.

Truman and Stimson and the members of his committee saw the bomb as a way to avoid this costly invasion. The question that remained was whether or not the bomb had to be dropped on a Japanese city to end the war. Might not a harmless demonstration of its awesome power persuade the Japanese to surrender?

Truman and his military advisers decided against a mere demonstration of the bomb. The fanaticism that the Japanese had shown in their conduct of the war led the American leaders to believe that a real blow in the form of a surprise attack was the surest path. The world had been at war for six years. For the past two years, the Allied powers had been in agreement that Japan and Ger-

many must surrender unconditionally. A negotiated peace was not acceptable, and, like the Germans, the Japanese were expected to fight long beyond the point at which their defeat was obvious. They would make the Allies pay the total price for total victory. Thus the American leaders decided to drop the bomb on a major Japanese city.

By early July, the team at Los Alamos was making final, frantic preparations to test the bomb. The site for the test was Alamogordo Air Base, an isolated location in the desert, two hundred miles

Secretary of War Henry L. Stimson

south of Los Alamos. Robert Oppenheimer's code name for the test site was "Trinity."

After two postponements, Groves and Oppenheimer scheduled the test for Monday, July 16, 4 A.M. Last-minute technical problems and bad weather threatened to cause another delay. Throughout most of the night of July 15–16, heavy rain battered the test site, the storm passing directly overhead at around 2:30 A.M.

By 4 A.M., however, the storm had broken, the wind had eased, and the sky had cleared. The test bomb was already in place at the top of a hundred-foot-high steel tower. Detonation had been rescheduled for 5:30 A.M. The scientists and technicians drew back to a control bunker about five miles from the bomb tower.

As the final minutes passed, the mood in the bunker grew very tense. Finally, at 5:29:45 A.M., the first man-made nuclear explosion lit up the pre-dawn New Mexico sky. A yellow-red fireball brighter than the sun slowly rose to a height of eight miles. The steel tower that the bomb was mounted on had been vaporized. The strength of the blast was equal to that of 20,000 tons—or 40 million pounds—of TNT. People saw the light from the explosion from three hundred miles away. The great scientific effort had borne brilliant but deadly fruit.

Core of the test bomb being loaded for transport to Alamogordo

Los Alamos Scientific Laboratory/AIP

Los Alamos Scientific Laboratory/AIP

Bombshell being raised to the top of the tower at Alamogordo

As the Oppenheimer team was busy preparing for the test at Alamogordo on July 15, Truman was arriving at Potsdam, Germany, for his first conference with Churchill and Stalin. The U.S. president, there to discuss the future of Europe and the terms of surrender for Japan, was eager for word of the "Trinity" test. Possession of the ultimate weapon would substantially improve his bargaining power with Stalin.

News of the successful test reached Potsdam late in the day on July 16. But the first coded messages provided no details. A full report of the bomb's awesome power finally arrived by courier plane at Potsdam on Saturday, July 21. Truman was suddenly a new man, possessed of enormous energy and self-confidence. He began to dictate terms to Stalin. Before the conference, Truman had decided to talk the Russians into joining the war against Japan. The bomb freed Truman from needing Russian help and from having to make further bargains with Stalin.

A few days later, Truman spoke privately to Stalin. He told the Russian leader that the United States "had a new weapon of unusual destructive force." Truman did not mention the word "atomic" and believed that Stalin had no clue to the real nature of the new weapon. Unknown to Truman, however, Stalin had been aware of the bomb project for some time. A member of the Los Alamos team of scientists, Klaus Fuchs, had been passing secret information to Soviet agents for two years. The Russians were using the stolen secrets to develop a bomb of their own.

On July 26, Truman made a final overture to the Japanese. He sent out a message from Potsdam, without consulting the Russians, again demanding the immediate and unconditional surrender of Japan. The Potsdam Declaration assured the Japanese that their economy, culture, and traditions would be kept intact if they surrendered. If they refused to surrender, Japan would be utterly destroyed. The bomb itself was not mentioned.

Four days later, July 30, the New York *Times* reported that Japan had officially turned down Truman's ultimatum.

At 1:37 A.M. on the night of August 5–6, 1945, three American B-29 bombers took off simultaneously from three sep-

arate runways on Tinian Island, in the Pacific. Each bomber headed for a different Japanese city: one to Hiroshima, another to Kokura, the third to Nagasaki. Their mission was to scout the weather conditions over the three principal targets for the atomic bomb.

A little more than an hour later, at 2:45 A.M., Colonel Paul Tibbets pushed forward the throttles of the B-29 he had named after his mother. The *Enola Gay* surged forward along the runway. Dangerously overweight, the plane used up more than two thirds of the runway without achieving takeoff speed. Captain Robert Lewis, the copilot, shouted to Tibbets that the plane was too heavy for takeoff. Tibbets didn't listen, and with almost no runway left, the *Enola Gay* got off the ground with just seconds to spare.

At 2:52 A.M., Deke Parsons, the chief weaponeer for Special Bombing Mission No. 13, headed for the *Enola Gay's* bomb bay. His job was to install the detonator in the first atomic bomb—code-named "Little Boy"—to be used in warfare. Parsons had decided to wait until the *Enola Gay* was airborne to arm the Little Boy because a crash on takeoff would have resulted in the total destruction of the air base on Tinian.

At 4:55 A.M., the *Enola Gay* was joined by two more B-29s assigned to make scientific tests and take photo-

Churchill, Truman, and Stalin at Potsdam

graphs. Together, the three planes flew in V-formation toward Japan.

At 7:25 A.M. Japanese time, the *Enola Gay* received a report from the weather plane that had already reached Hiroshima, the primary target. The cloud cover was sparse and not a problem. *Enola Gay* was advised, "Bomb primary."

At 8:09, with Hiroshima in view, Tibbets announced to the plane's crew that the bombing run was about to begin. He ordered the crew to have their special goggles ready on their foreheads.

"When the countdown starts," Tibbets said, "pull the goggles over your eyes and leave them there until after the flash."

At 8:13 Tibbets turned control of the *Enola Gay* over to Major Thomas Ferebee, the bombardier. The B-29 was flying at a speed of 285 miles per hour, at an altitude of 31,600 feet. Ferebee stared down through the bomb sight at a target familiar to him from careful study of aerial photographs. He easily identified the seven tributaries of the Ota River that form the six islands of Hiroshima. Then he watched for the Aioi Bridge, the aiming point for the bomb.

The B-29 bomber Enola Gay

Smithsonian Institution

U.S. Air Force

Ground and flight crew of the Enola Gay *at Tinian Island. Colonel Paul Tibbets, the pilot, is standing at center, in flight overalls and dark cap.*

"I've got it," he said.

At seventeen seconds past 8:15, the automatically operated bomb-bay doors of the *Enola Gay* swung open. The bomb, nearly 10,000 pounds, dropped through the doors, and the plane, suddenly lightened, lurched upward.

Tibbets immediately took back the controls and banked the plane violently to the right until he had changed course by 150 degrees.

"Make sure those goggles are on," Tibbets ordered through the plane's intercom.

At about 2,000 feet from the ground, the bomb burst into an enormous fireball with a temperature hotter than the surface of the sun. Granite melted. The shadows of people walking the streets of Hiroshima were imprinted on walls. A shock wave pushed out from the center of the blast with such force that build-

U.S. Air Force

Aerial view of Hiroshima after the blast. The city is made up of six side-by-side islands connected by hundreds of bridges.

ings up to three miles away were flattened instantly.

Tibbets later described what he and his crew saw from the *Enola Gay*. "[There was] a mushroom cloud growing up, and we watched it blossom. And down below it the thing reminded me more of a boiling pot of tar than any other description I can give it. It was black and boiling underneath with a steam haze on top of it."

Of the 350,000 residents of Hiroshima, some 130,000 were killed instantly or doomed to die from injuries or radiation received during the blast. One bomb laid waste to the entire city. Of the people who had been within 1,500 feet of ground zero (the point directly over which the bomb exploded), 88 percent were dead by the end of the day.

Those who survived the initial blast were thrust into a living hell on earth. Many were blackened with burns. Many were bleeding from wounds. Many were blinded. Many were buried beneath rubble. All across Hiroshima, isolated fires were ignited by the heat from the blast. Winds soon whipped these individual fires into a single, terrifying firestorm that ignited telephone poles as though they were kitchen matches.

As the day wore on, scorched survivors slowly made their way from the center of the city. Many cried out for water to ease the pain of burns or to cure a horrible thirst. Most were in a daze, as if walking in their sleep.

Over the next day or so, the first signs of another deadly aspect of the

One of the bomb's many victims

Defense Audiovisual Agency

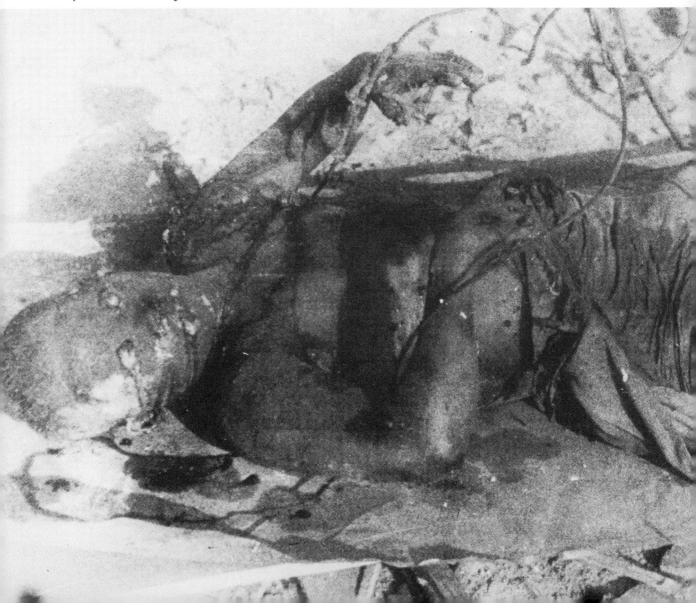

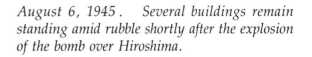

Defense Audiovisual Agency

bomb were becoming apparent. Beyond its destructive force and brutal heat, the explosion had released an incredible level of lethal gamma rays. Radiation sickness began to kill thousands who had managed to survive the actual blast. People who had escaped death from burns or injuries were suddenly suffering from repeated vomiting and internal bleeding. As the sickness progressed, their hair fell out and they suffered terrible fevers, and, for the most part, they died.

Hiroshima was a last jolt of horror amid all the many horrors of a world at war.

August 6, 1945. Several buildings remain standing amid rubble shortly after the explosion of the bomb over Hiroshima.

4

THE WAR ENDS

To the present day, most Americans have difficulty understanding Japanese culture and society, and in 1945, the people of the United States understood even less. Americans were unfamiliar with the everyday values of Japanese society, and they had been greatly influenced by wartime propaganda that had portrayed the "Jap" as a brutal savage.

Indeed, the Japanese had inspired hatred in the United States in two significant ways. One was the surprise attack on Pearl Harbor, which brought the U.S. into the war, and the other was the mistreatment of American prisoners of war by the Japanese. These matters horrified the American public and affected the decisions of U.S. military and political leaders.

Times Square, New York, August 15, 1945. Hundreds of thousands celebrate "VJ-Day" in the shadow of a Statue of Liberty replica.

The Japanese were a people with a profound code of personal honor. This code of honor went hand in hand with a devotion to the emperor of Japan, who was regarded by the people as nearly a god. It was the code of honor that called for the Japanese military to fight to the death. It also called for those who failed in their duties to commit ritual suicide, or *seppuku* (often mistakenly referred to in the West as *hara-kiri*). And although the number of actual *kamikaze* missions by Japanese pilots became exaggerated in American minds, the nature of the act itself was enough to cause Americans to fear the enemy's willingness to fight to the death.

These aspects of the Japanese war effort influenced Truman's decision to use the bomb on Hiroshima. The president believed that the overwhelming destructive force of the bomb was needed to bring the Japanese to surrender and to spare the further loss of American soldiers.

UPI/Bettmann Archive

U.S. Marines storm from their landing craft and hit the beach at Iwo Jima, February 1945. The Americans captured the island, but casualties were high.

Hiroshima did not, as it turns out, force the immediate surrender of the Japanese. The highest level of Japan's leadership were desperate to avoid surrender and hoped that a peace treaty could be arranged at the last moment. A frantic diplomatic effort was made to get the Soviets to act as a go-between with the United States. The Japanese clearly wished to remain a sovereign, unoccupied nation.

But this was not to be. The American leaders, though willing to allow Japan to continue its national traditions, wanted to put an end to Japan as a military threat. They had no desire to destroy Japanese society, enslave the people, or punish them inordinately. But the memory of how quickly and vengefully Germany had rearmed after World War I was fresh. The American leaders did not want to end this war with a peace treaty and then be forced to fight Japan again twenty years hence.

When the Japanese did not surrender immediately after the bombing of Hiroshima, the decision was made to drop a second atomic bomb on Japan. The date would be August 9, three days after Hiroshima, and the target was to be the port city of Nagasaki.

Again, unspeakable death and suffering resulted. The number of people killed was estimated at 70,000, with as many wounded.

The day before the Nagasaki bombing, the Russians had declared war on Japan. In Tokyo, the Supreme War Council convened just as Nagasaki was being destroyed. Even the news of Nagasaki and the Russian declaration of war did not convince the militarist faction on the council that it was useless to fight on.

Later in the evening of August 9, having failed to reach a decision on peace or war, the council went to meet with Emperor Hirohito in his bunker. Breaking a tradition that the emperor not lower himself to making political decisions, Hirohito advised the council that the war must end.

"The time has come when we must bear the unbearable," he said, referring to the American demand for unconditional surrender. The ministers present agreed to sign an acceptance of the Potsdam Declaration (the Allies' official demand for Japanese surrender) with the understanding that the supreme authority of the emperor be recognized and retained.

The provision concerning the emperor held up the final agreement by Truman and the other Allies. In Washington, Truman and his advisers drafted a reply that would satisfy both the Allies' terms of surrender and Japan's wish that the emperor's traditional role in Japanese life be recognized. The crucial sentence in the reply, sent on August 11, was "The authority of the Emperor and the Japanese Government shall be subject to the Supreme Commander of the Allied powers."

Once again, this was not immediately acceptable to the more militant ministers in Tokyo. Three more days of indecision passed. The emperor decided to move again to break the impasse. He called the ministers together and insisted that they accept the terms of surrender. At last, the ministers agreed to bow to the wishes of the emperor. Hirohito made a recording that would be broadcast to the Japanese people. The recording was an announcement that the war was over.

Before the broadcast, a group of rebellious army officers attempted to stop the announcement. After closing off the grounds of the Imperial Palace, they

National Archives

Emperor Hirohito

47

tried to find the emperor's recording, to destroy it. The recording had been carefully hidden and was not found, and the officers were eventually persuaded to withdraw from the palace grounds.

At noon on August 15, 1945, the emperor's message was finally heard by the Japanese people. In his statement, the emperor said that the atomic bomb made it impossible to fight any longer. "The enemy has begun to employ a new and cruel bomb, whose power to do damage is indeed incalculable, taking the toll of many innocent lives. Should we continue to fight, it would not only result in an ultimate collapse and obliteration of the Japanese nation but would also lead to the total extinction of human civilization. . . ."

The end of the war in the Pacific was greeted with celebration across the United States. For many, the most frightening conflict in history had come to a close. But it was not long before the jubilation of victory could no longer dispel sober thoughts about the future.

Hiroshima had not only signaled the end of humankind's most destructive war; it had also marked the beginning of an era in which the world's next war would likely be its last. Emperor Hirohito had not exaggerated when he said that the bomb could lead to the "total extinction of human civilization."

At Hiroshima and Nagasaki, the United States had introduced the world to the "ultimate weapon." But there was one hitch. The ultimate weapon tran-scended war, went far beyond right and wrong, made the concept of "victory" in the next world war instantly out of date.

When Winston Churchill first heard reports of the bomb's terrible power, after the Alamogordo test, he compared it to biblical prophecies about the end of the world. Now the stories about tens of thousands of maimed and burned people, about the dead and the dying, began to reveal the final victory as an awesome contradiction: The long-sought-after end to this hateful war, which had inspired mass destruction and the torture and extermination of millions of people, had left as a legacy a weapon more awful than the war itself.

No sooner had the first two atomic bombs fallen on Japan than religious and social leaders in the United States called on President Truman to discontinue its use. The president's own statement on Hiroshima had referred to the bomb as a "harnessing of the basic power of the universe." This was something of an innocent misstatement on Truman's part. Although the atomic bomb may well involve the "basic power of the universe," it is far from a "harnessing" of that power. It would have been more accurate if Truman had called it the *unleashing* of the basic power of the universe. "Harnessing" imples "under control"; "unleashing" implies "out of control."

Harry Truman, from the day he assumed the presidency, kept a sign on his desk that read "The Buck Stops Here." That sign meant that the president took responsibility for the policies, decisions, and problems of his administration. Truman never once ducked responsibility for having ordered the nuclear attack on Hiroshima. Years later he said that he still had no regrets about that decision. As a result, he has often borne the brunt of criticism from those who see Hiroshima as a crime against humanity.

The atomic bomb had been rushed into existence by dedicated people who feared that the Germans would have it first. Though Germany fell before the bomb was ready, it had earlier been decided, by Roosevelt, that the bomb might be deployed in Japan but not in Germany. Some contend that as a nation

A British sailor celebrates VJ-Day in New York City.

UPI/Bettmann Archive

Defense Audiovisual Agency

September 2, 1945. The Japanese chief of staff signs the surrender agreement as MacArthur (far left) and other senior Allied officers look on.

of primarily European descendants, the U.S. and its leadership would have been reluctant to use such devastating force in the "Old Country" but had fewer qualms about using it against the less familiar, greatly feared, and deeply hated Asians. Others point to the fire-bombing of Dresden in February of 1945 as evidence that the U.S. was willing to use maximum force against the Germans.

In the spring of 1945, with the fall of Germany, the war-weary Allies had turned their attention to the defeat of Japan. The invasion that was being planned might have cost hundreds of thousands, or even millions, of American and Japanese lives. A vision of what was best for the future was necessarily overshadowed by the hard facts of a long-drawn-out war. Given the opportunity to end the war with one brutal stroke, Truman took it.

With the war in the Pacific brought to an abrupt end, Truman was left in a stronger position to deal with the Soviets. Stalin was interested in bringing as much territory as possible under the Soviet sphere of influence. He had agreed to send a large army to help invade Japan, if such an invasion were to take place, but in return he wanted to be allowed to occupy one of the main Japanese islands. Stalin even requested such a concession after the war, but Truman rejected the idea out of hand.

AFTERWORD

THE NUCLEAR AGE

Before the first test of the atomic bomb at Alamogordo, it had already occurred to Niels Bohr, one of the fathers of atomic physics, that the world might soon be threatened by a nuclear-arms race. Bohr met with both Roosevelt and Churchill and urged them to avert an arms race by placing the bomb under international control. This implied that all knowledge of the bomb would be shared with the Soviet Union, the chief competitor with the United States for world power and influence.

At the time, the war made such an idealistic plan seem almost impossible. In the middle of a brutal struggle, a scientist was suggesting that the Americans and British share the most devastating knowledge on the planet with a country that, although an ally

during the war, would almost surely be an enemy afterward. Bohr was asking these two powerful leaders to look beyond the mists of a confused world. He was asking them to travel a new and untried road before the time was right. The great scientist's advice was, of course, not taken.

After the war, the United States did make a proposal before the United Nations to place atomic weapons under the control of an international agency. The plan was presented in 1946, but the Soviets rejected it, unable to accept the provision for the on-site inspection of its territory that would allow the agency to enforce its rules.

The nuclear-arms race so feared by Niels Bohr is today the most solemn fact of modern life. When the first two

Divided Berlin; November 1961

atomic weapons were used against Japan, they were the only two that were ready. More were in production, but there was no such thing as a "nuclear arsenal." Today, the worldwide arsenal of nuclear weapons, held primarily by the United States and the Soviet Union, totals more than 50,000 warheads. Together, these weapons have more than 1.5 million times the power of the Hiroshima bomb. Their total destructive force is in the neighborhood of 20 billion *tons* of TNT. They can be delivered to targets by long-range bombers, air- and ground-launched missiles, and submarine-launched missiles.

A nuclear war between the two superpowers would be concluded in a few hours. The result would be the destruction of most inhabited regions of the earth's Northern Hemisphere. But the effects would not end there. So many nuclear explosions in so short a time could devastate the entire planet. All regions of the world might be enshrouded in a cloud of nuclear dust. The temperature around the globe would fall rapidly, and the entire earth would be poisoned by massive radioactive fallout.

How did the single, horrible reality of Hiroshima turn into a potential horror 1½ million times as powerful? The answer lies in the destructive traditions of human civilization itself. The bombing of Hiroshima constituted a basic change in the course of human history, but world politics has not yet caught up to the challenge of nuclear power. For centuries, the settlement of disputes has frequently been accomplished on the field of battle. Warfare is an ever-evolving "art," with its champions elevated to high position and sometimes heroic stature. In many respects, war has become the ultimate test of loyalty, of patriotism: Few acts are deemed more honorable than the defense of one's country against an enemy.

At the beginning of this century, the rapid development of new industries and technologies was transforming human society. Suddenly the oceans were conquered by coal- and steam-powered ships. Railroads connected city with city and, in Europe, country with country. The automobile, the airplane, and the wireless radio made the world, in effect, a smaller and more familiar place.

The dark side of modern progress was that it brought about the perfection of powerful instruments of war. Machine guns, poison gas, tanks, submarines, battleships, airplanes, aircraft carriers, guided missiles, and other sophisticated weapons have figured prominently in the wars of this century. They were the inventions of people and nations in conflict with one another, ready to solve their conflicts through war.

The great developments of industry, science, and technology had shot out far ahead of developments in world politics. Europe, in particular, was a swarm of similar but hostile cultures. World Wars I and II were the product of centuries of European turmoil.

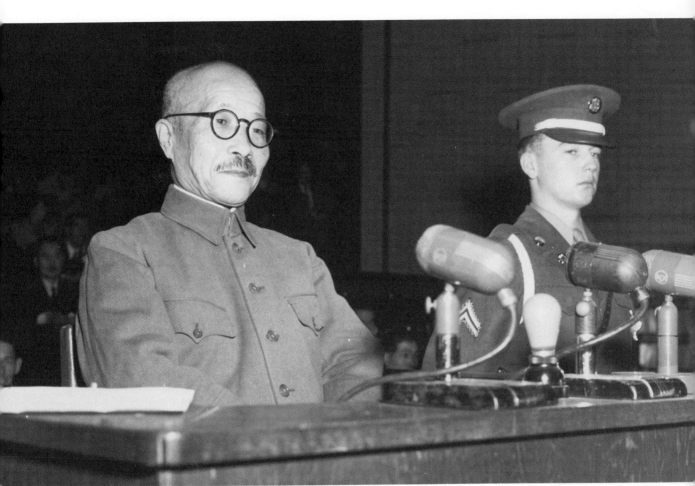

Defense Audiovisual Agency

Former prime minister Tojo during testimony at his trial for war crimes. He was found guilty by the Allied court and executed.

The United States had entered both of these conflicts reluctantly. The American tradition, never perfectly applied, had been to remain neutral in European wars. In the Second World War, the Nazis were too threatening for the United States to ignore, and the surprise attack on Pearl Harbor by the Japanese was the almost welcome excuse Franklin Roosevelt needed to exert American power in a embattled world.

When the war ended, the United States and the Soviet Union emerged as the two great competing powers. In Europe, the two sides drew up the battle lines of what is known as the "Cold War." Stalin established "satellite" governments, under the control of the Soviet Communist Party, in Poland, East Germany, Albania, Czechoslovakia, Hungary, Rumania, and Bulgaria. The United States, with its allies Great Britain and France, worked strenuously to prevent Soviet communism from spreading further, into Italy, Austria, Greece, and Turkey. Truman pushed through Congress a plan to help rebuild Europe after the war. The Marshall Plan, named for Secretary of State George Marshall, won much support and many friends for the United States. Ultimately, the countries of Western Europe joined the United States in the North Atlantic Treaty Organization (NATO), which sought to guarantee the security of its members.

The Cold War was also alive in Asia, where China was enveloped in the communist revolution led by Mao Zedong. Korea was partitioned, with the northern part coming under a Russian-backed communist government. Another communist revolution was soon in progress in Southeast Asia, in the newly formed nation of Vietnam. The United States, meanwhile, occupied Japan and worked steadily to reestablish its economy and provide for its national defense. Japan has since become one of the most successful industrial nations in the world and a trusted ally of the United States.

The first major military conflict of the Cold War began in 1950 when communist forces from North Korea invaded South Korea. The United States responded by leading a United Nations force in what was called a "police action." This war ended in 1953 in a virtual stalemate. In 1949, just a year before the fighting had begun in Korea, the nu-

clear-arms race had accelerated when the Soviets tested their first atomic bomb.

In 1950, Truman approved the development of the more powerful hydrogen bomb. The scientists had this new nuclear weapon ready in 1952. Only a year later, the Russians announced that they, too, had an H-bomb.

From the time of the division of Germany—at the 1945 Potsdam Conference—into Soviet-backed East and Allied-backed West Germany, the Cold War has moved from crisis to crisis and the nuclear arms race has continued. In 1948, the Soviets blocked all land and water routes between West Germany and its zone of Berlin. (Berlin is located geographically in East Germany.) In response, the Western powers began to fly supplies into West Berlin. This "airlift" lasted until the autumn of 1949 and helped solidify West Germany's claim to its portion of the great city.

Twelve years after the airlift, in 1961, East Germany built a wall to separate its zone of Berlin from the zone that belonged to West Germany. This was done to prevent the steady migration of refugees from East to West. Tensions ran high as the wall was erected, and there was fear in West Germany, in the United States, and among the other NATO powers that the East Germans, with the help of the Soviets, might try to overrun

The "mushroom cloud" of a hydrogen bomb tested at Bikini Atoll, in the Pacific, in 1956

MacArthur served as supreme commander of the Allied Occupational Government of Japan from 1945 to 1951.

West Berlin. No military action was taken during this crisis, but the side-by-side existence of the "two Germanys" has continued as a trouble spot in the ongoing Cold War.

In 1962, the Soviet Union and the United States had a major confrontation over the island country of Cuba in the Caribbean, ninety miles off the southern shore of Florida. Fidel Castro, the leader of the revolution in Cuba, had established a communist government there in 1959. In April 1961, about 2,000 anti-Castro Cuban refugees backed by the U.S. government invaded Cuba with the intention of overthrowing Castro's government. The invasion was repelled at a point on Cuba's southern coast called the Bay of Pigs, and the mission ended in failure, with many of the invaders taken prisoner. Then, in October 1962, United States reconnaissance planes confirmed that the Soviets were building missile bases in Cuba.

President John F. Kennedy told the Russians that the weapons had to be removed. Kennedy ordered the navy to surround Cuba and prevent Soviet ships carrying missiles from delivering them to Cuban ports. Kennedy carried on negotiations with Nikita Khrushchev, the Soviet premier, through an exchange of letters. The crisis reached a peak as a Soviet ship approached American ships in the Caribbean.

Just as a confrontation seemed unavoidable, the Soviet ship stopped and turned back. Later, the Russians agreed to remove the missiles in exchange for a promise from Kennedy that the U.S. would not invade Cuba. The compromise worked, and the crisis ended. But the world had had a glimpse of the "nuclear brink."

The superpowers seemed to rebound from the Cuban confrontation with a fresh sense of the importance of peace. In 1963 they managed to agree to the Nuclear Test-Ban Treaty, which prohibits the testing of nuclear weapons in the earth's atmosphere. Still, cordial relations were not in the offing.

The Vietnam War, in which the United States was heavily involved between 1965 and 1974, was the most recent military conflict involving the superpowers. The Americans had, at one time, more than half a million troops

Lawrence Radiation Laboratory/AIP

Physicist Edward Teller, who was primarily responsible for development of the H-Bomb

fighting on the side of South Vietnam. The Soviet Union supported communist North Vietnam, the eventual victor in the war, with weapons and economic aid. Both superpowers, however, were extremely careful about avoiding a direct confrontation with each other. Oddly enough, even as Vietnam continued, a friendlier attitude between the powers began. This was the period of *détente* (French for "relaxation") that was initiated during the administration of President Richard Nixon.

As the 1970s progressed, however, the Soviets again initiated a buildup of both conventional and nuclear arms. American leaders feared that the Soviets might achieve superiority over the United States in its nuclear weaponry, and by the early 1980s the United States had responded with an expansion of its military spending and arms development.

The policy of both the United States and the Soviet Union regarding nuclear warfare is called "deterrence." This means that should one side consider unleashing a nuclear attack on the other, the attacker must understand that the other side will launch a counterattack that would destroy the aggressor nation. Thus, both powers are "deterred" from considering such an attack.

For some time, the Americans and the Soviets have made attempts, not entirely unsuccessful, to talk about arms control. In 1972, they signed the first Strategic Arms Limitation Treaty (SALT). It seems, however, that this treaty only changed the course of the arms race, in that both sides turned to the development of weapons not covered by the treaty. SALT II, a later treaty, has been observed for the most part by both sides, in spite of the fact that it has never been ratified by the U.S. Senate, which must, according to the Constitution, approve all treaties.

New talks on arms control have been held off and on, and talks on arms reduction have been proposed. The superpowers continue to grapple with the problem of nuclear weapons, but the world is still waiting for a major breakthrough.

Each time the leaders or the people of the world discuss nuclear weapons, they must inevitably refer back to Hiroshima. There lies the living example of a fate too ominous to comprehend, a symbol of what must never be allowed to happen again. There lies humankind's severest test, its greatest challenge.

INDEX

Page numbers in *italics* indicate illustrations

SUGGESTED READING

BRADLEY, JOHN H. *The Second World War: Asia and the Pacific.* The West Point History Series. Wayne, N.J.: Avery Publishing, 1984.

HERSEY, JOHN. *Hiroshima.* New York: Bantam, 1946.

NATKIEL, RICHARD. *Atlas of Battles: Strategy and Tactics, Civil War to Present.* 5th chapter, "World War II," pp. 57–135. New York: Military Press/Bison Books, 1984.

SHERWIN, MARTIN J. *A World Destroyed: The Atomic Bomb and the Grand Alliance.* New York: Knopf, 1975.

WYDEN, PETER. *Day One: Before Hiroshima and After.* New York: Simon & Schuster, 1984.

2 3 4 5 6 7 8 9 10—JDL—93 92 91 90 89 88 87 86

PROPERTY OF
CHICAGO BOARD OF EDUCATION
DONALD L. MORRILL SCHOOL

940.54
MAC
  McPhillips, Martin
    Hiroshima

DATE DUE			

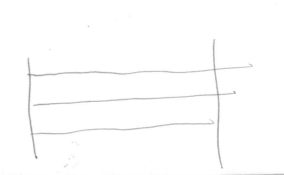